Say *It With* Style™

Perfect Quotes for Every Card-Making Occasion

EDITED BY TANYA FOX

HOUSE of
WHITE
BIRCHES

PUBLISHERS
SINCE 1947

Say *It With* Style™

EDITOR	Tanya Fox
ART DIRECTOR	Brad Snow
DESIGNER	Jeff Amstutz, a2zdesign.com
PUBLISHING SERVICES DIRECTOR	Brenda Gallmeyer
ASSOCIATE EDITOR	Sue Reeves
ASSISTANT ART DIRECTOR	Nick Pierce
COPY SUPERVISOR	Michelle Beck
COPY EDITORS	Mary O'Donnell, Judy Weatherford
PHOTOGRAPHY SUPERVISOR	Tammy Christian
PHOTOGRAPHY	Matthew Owen
PHOTOGRAPHY STYLIST	Tammy Steiner
GRAPHIC ARTS SUPERVISOR	Ronda Bechinski
PRODUCTION ASSISTANTS	Marj Morgan, Judy Neuenschwander

Printed in the USA
First Printing: 2008 in China
Library of Congress Control Number: 2008923500
Hard Cover ISBN: 978-1-59217-180-4
Soft Cover ISBN: 978-1-59217-227-6

DRGbooks.com

4 5 6 7 8 9

WELCOME

Dear crafting friend,

I've heard it said time after time by my card-making friends, "It's so easy to come up with the design for the front of the card, but what do I do with the inside?" Where do we find those perfect words to convey the thought or purpose of the card? And so began the journey of creating a helpful resource to assist my friends.

In this book, you'll find a wonderful collection of simple phrases, heartwarming sentiments and thought-provoking quotations that are perfect for use in handmade cards and other memory crafts as well. Arranged in alphabetical order of event, the quotations

 and sentiments are grouped by some of the most popular card-making occasions. Perhaps you are looking for a humorous quip to include in a card for your best friend, or maybe a family member is celebrating a milestone birthday. Could someone close to you use a few uplifting words of encouragement? We've tried to include a broad variety of phrases to encompass as many life-events and occasions as possible.

There are quotations that make me laugh out loud, some that touch my heart, and still others that have a profound impact on how I view the everyday events of life. I have to agree with Marlene Dietrich, the legendary motion-picture actress: Finding these quotes has been a joy. My hope is that as you read through these pages and use the words to bless others through your handmade cards, that you'll find a little of that joy as well.

Tanya

I love quotations because it is a joy to find thoughts one might have, beautifully expressed with much authority by someone recognized wiser than oneself.

—Marlene Dietrich

 CONTENTS

May your walls know joy; may every room hold laughter and every window open to great possibility.

— Mary Ann Radmacher

'Twas not my lips you kissed, but my soul.

—Judy Garland

Birthdays

50

Just remember, once you're over the hill you begin to pick up speed.
-CHARLES SCHULZ

Birthday wishes to a special friend,
for lots of joys, both big and small!

There is no old age. There is, as there always was, just you.

—Carol Matthau

Happy birthday with a cherry on top!

Light the candles.

May your birthday be as full of love as you are!

You get better
every day!

**May this day
be as special
as you are.**

To be 70 years
young is sometimes far
more cheerful
and hopeful than
to be 40 years old.

—Oliver Wendell Holmes

A birthday is just
the first day of
another 365-day
journey around the
sun. Enjoy the trip!

Birthdays

It's your birthday ...
so have a ball!

Sweetest birthday wishes for the sweetest gal around!

Thinking of you on your special day and hoping this year brings you joy, peace and much happiness.

One thing is certain, and I have always known it—the joys of my life have nothing to do with age.

—May Sarton

A birthday wish for you: May all your birthday wishes come true!

Someone like you should be celebrated every day.

Wish: the heart's desire.

May your every wish come true.

There is still no cure for the common birthday.

—John Glenn

Wishing you every little thing your heart desires ... and every big thing too!

Hope your birthday is bright with love and laughter.

Growing old is mandatory; growing up is optional.

—Chili Davis

Party 'til the cows come home!

You're not 40, you're 18 with 22 years experience.

Hope you reel in the catch of the day ... all good birthday wishes!

Just remember, once you're over the hill you begin to pick up speed. —Charles Schultz

Aging is not "lost youth," but a new stage of opportunity and strength.

—Betty Friedan

May song and cheer fill your special day and the whole year through.

Birthdays

Don't think of it as another year older ... think of it as another year of shopping!

Another belief of mine; that everyone else my age is an adult, whereas I am merely in disguise.

—Margaret Atwood

Birthdays are good for you; the more you have the longer you live!

Just buzzin' by with a birthday hi!

I thought and thought ... and then I forgot. Happy belated birthday.

May your birthday be as special as you are.

Happy: a feeling of giddiness or joy.

Wishing you a most delightful birthday!

Youth is the gift of nature, but age is a work of art.

—Stanislaw Lec

*Youth would be an ideal state
if it came a little later in life.*
—Herbert Asquith

Celebrate your birthday with your flag flying high.

You're how old?

Wishing you a beautiful day to remember.

So many candles, so little cake.

Indulge yourself on your birthday ... order dessert first!

When grace is joined by wrinkles, it is adorable. There is an unspeakable dawn in happy old age.
—Victor Hugo

I still have a full deck; I just shuffle slower now.

May you enjoy blessings today and every day!

No matter how old you are, there's always something good to look forward to.

—Lynn Johnston

May today and every day in the year ahead bring you something to enjoy.

Grow old along with me! The best is yet to be.

—Robert Browning

Happy birthday to the sweetest person I know!

Old age is no place for sissies. —Bette Davis

Oh no! A gray hare!

The joy is in the journey.

Pouring out abundant good wishes for a happy, happy birthday.

Old age is not so bad when you consider the alternatives.

—Maurice Chevalier

May you live to be 100 years with one extra year to repent.

How old would you be if you didn't know how old you were?

—Satchel Paige

I think age is a very high price to pay for maturity.

—Tom Stoppard

You don't stop laughing because you grow old. You grow old because you stop laughing.

—Michael Pritchard

Wish big!

Hope your day is filled with sunshine and smiles!

To me, old age is always 15 years older than I am.

—Bernard M. Baruch

Pamper yourself and celebrate in style!

In our dreams we are always young. —Sarah Louise Delany

I'm 60 years of age. That's 16 Celsius.

—George Carlin

Sure, I'm for helping the elderly. I'm going to be old myself some day.

—Lillian Carter

You know you've reached middle age when a doctor, not a policeman, tells you to slow down.

—Author unknown

Middle age is when your age starts to show around your middle.

—Bob Hope

Hope you have a "honey" of a birthday!

Wishing you a basketful of joy on your special day!

Have a Magical Day!

Middle age is when you've met so many people that every new person you meet reminds you of someone else. —Ogden Nash

Hope your day is filled with everything you love.

Age is no barrier. It's a limitation you put on your mind.

—Jackie Joyner-Kersee

Today I celebrate you!

Birthday hugs and wishes.

Age is strictly a case of mind over matter. If you don't mind, it doesn't matter.

—Jack Benny

The secret of staying young is to live honestly, eat slowly and lie about your age.

—Lucille Ball

You take the cake! Happy birthday to the sweetest person I know.

Wisdom doesn't necessarily come with age. Sometimes age just shows up all by itself.

—Tom Wilson

Sending you a little something wrapped in a whole lot of love.

Inflation is when you pay $15 for the $10 haircut you used to get for $5 when you had hair. —Sam Ewing

You are only young once,
but you can stay immature indefinitely.
—Ogden Nash

Old age is like everything else.
To make a success of it, you've got to start young.
—Fred Astaire

It's all about you.

*To get back my youth
I would do anything
in the world, except
take exercise, get up
early, or be respectable.*
—Oscar Wilde

We know we're getting old when the only thing we want for our birthday is not to be reminded of it.

CELEBRATE: to perform; to commemorate with festivity; to honor publicly; to have a good time.

Warmest Wishes

Middle age is having a choice between two temptations and choosing the one that'll get you home earlier.

—Dan Bennett

Inside every older person is a younger person wondering what happened.

—Jennifer Yane

The really frightening thing about middle age is the knowledge that you'll grow out of it.

—Doris Day

Youth is a wonderful thing. What a crime to waste it on children.

—George Bernard Shaw

The first sign of maturity is the discovery that the volume knob also turns to the left.

—Jerry M. Wright

They say that age is all in your mind.
The trick is keeping it from creeping down into your body.

—author unknown

Children

Your precious baby,
So tiny and new,
Is a miracle of love,
From God to you.

Each day of our lives we make deposits in the memory banks of our children.

—Charles R. Swindoll, *The Strong Family*

Hush little baby, don't you cry.

You will always be your child's favorite toy.

—Vicki Lansky

Babies are little angels from above.

Children are a gift from God.

One little baby, many happy hearts.

Every child begins
the world again.

—Henry David Thoreau

**What's sweeter
than cookies?
Why a sweet
new baby of
course.**

A baby is a blessing,
A gift of Heaven above,
A precious little angel,
To cherish and to love.

Congratulations
on your precious
bundle of joy!

The most precious gifts are those that are small.

A baby is born with a need to be loved and never outgrows it.

A new little someone
Sent from above,
Full of sweetness and wonder,
Bundled in love.

There is only one pretty child in the world, and every mother has it.

—Chinese proverb

Boy: a noise with dirt on it.

It would seem that something which means poverty, disorder and violence every single day should be avoided entirely, but the desire to beget children is a natural urge.

—Phyllis Diller

A daughter is such a joy.

Childhood should be a journey, not a race.

Insanity is hereditary—you get it from your kids.

—Sam Levenson

Children are a great comfort in your old age—and they help you reach it faster too.

—Lionel Kauffman

Congratulations on your new little miracle!

A baby is a bundle of joy.

Babies are blessings from heaven.

Babies are life's most precious gift.

Adoption is when a child grew in its mommy's heart instead of her tummy.

—author unknown

Straight from heaven up above, here is a baby for us to love.

It sometimes happens, even in the best of families, that a baby is born. This is not necessarily cause for alarm. The important thing is to keep your wits about you and borrow some money.

—Elinor Goulding Smith

Setting a good example for your children takes all the fun out of middle age.

—William Feather

Roses round the door. Babies on the floor. Who could ask for more?

Babies are blessings from above, they fill our hearts with lots of love.

Special delivery

Congratulations on your sweet baby!

Every baby needs a lap.

—Henry Robin

Your precious baby, so tiny and new, Is a miracle of love, from God to you.

Making the decision to have a child is momentous. It is to decide forever to have your heart go walking around outside your body.

—Elizabeth Stone

A son is such a joy.

Babies are such a nice way to start people.
—Don Herrold

No earthly joys could bring more pleasure, than a little girl to love and treasure.

Always kiss your children good night— even if they're already asleep.
—H. Jackson Brown Jr.

A child enters your home and for the next 20 years makes so much noise you can hardly stand it. The child departs, leaving the house so silent you think you are going mad.
—John Andrew Holmes

Bundle of boy.

A baby is God's opinion that the world should go on.
—Carl Sandburg

#

Don't worry that children never listen to you; worry that they are always watching you.

—Robert Fulghum

Always end the name of your child with a vowel, so that when you yell, the name will carry.

—Bill Cosby

A baby is a blank check, made payable to the human race.

—Barbara Christine Seifert

Even when freshly washed and relieved of all obvious confections, children tend to be sticky.

—Fran Lebowitz

Babies are always more trouble than you thought—and more wonderful.

—Charles Osgood

When my kids become wild and unruly, I use a nice, safe playpen. When they're finished, I climb out.

—Erma Bombeck

Now the thing about having a baby—and I can't be the first person to have noticed this—is that thereafter you have it.

—Jean Kerr

If your kids are giving you a headache, follow the directions on the aspirin bottle, especially the part that says "keep away from children." —Susan Savannah

A new baby is like the beginning of all things—wonderful hope, a dream of possibilities.

—Eda LeShan

The cleaning and scrubbing will wait till tomorrow,

For children grow up, as I've learned to my sorrow,

So quiet down, cobwebs. Dust, go to sleep.

I'm rocking my baby, and babies don't keep.

—Ruth Hulburt Hamilton

To bring up a child in the way he should go, travel that way yourself once in a while.

—Josh Billings

Bundle of joy.

Christmas

may the light
that shone in Bethlehem
shine in your
heart
THIS Christmas

Who needs Santa? ...
I have Grandma

Wishing you
sparkle,
Wishing you cheer,
For a bright
merry Christmas
And a happy
new year.

Sending you greetings with best wishes for Christmas and the New Year.

Thinking of you with love this holiday season.

May Christmas blessings flock to you and your loved ones.

Warm thoughts and wishes keep us close in heart.

Come let us adore Him.

Sharing our Christmas together.

Wishing you a Christmas wrapped in joy
and filled with love and laughter.

The stockings were hung by the chimney with care.

Christmas is holly with berries of red
and the heavenly fragrance of warm gingerbread.

Hark! The herald angels sing.

Celebrate the season of love, peace and joy.

It is Christmas
in the heart that puts
Christmas in the air.

Gather with those you love to truly celebrate the season.

Plenty of wishes
are coming your
way to wish
you a wonderful
holiday.

May the gentle
gifts of the season
fill your heart with
peace and joy.

Warm winter wishes for a cozy holiday season and a wonderful new year.

May your home be filled with love and laughter this Christmas.

Reindeer crossing.

Life is worth living,
Dreams do come true,
If we keep the Christmas spirit,
The whole year through.

—author unknown

May your home be filled with the love of family and friends as you celebrate this season of togetherness.

Rejoice this Christmas for all the Lord has given you.

Wishing you a blessed Christmas.

Rejoicing with you in the miracle of Christmas.

Peace and plenty, love and joy,
may all of these be yours.

Merry Christmas from our house to yours.

Oh Come All Ye Faithful

Wishing that all the goodness and gladness of the holidays fill your heart with happiness that lasts throughout the year.

May you find joy in the season, the fellowship of friends and close family.

Friendship is the thread that ties all hearts together at Christmastime.

Amid the hustle and bustle of Christmas, may you be surrounded by the love and laughter of all those you hold dear.

May you and your loved ones be blessed with love and laughter throughout the holiday season.

Wishing you the warmth of home and the joy this season brings.

Happy ho-ho!

Glory to God in the highest and peace to his people on earth.

Remember the reason for the season.

May the light that shone in Bethlehem shine in your heart this Christmas.

Here comes Santa, making a list, checking it twice.

There's no place like home for the holidays.

Believe in the
magic of Christmas.

**May all
your holiday
memories
be warm
and bright.**

Wishing you
the happiest
of holidays
and a wonderful
new year.

A great big armful
of Christmas
wishes is being
sent your way.

'Twas the night before Christmas.

May the loving traditions of Christmas be yours
for the holidays and all the year through.

North Pole Bed & Breakfast

Rockin' around the Christmas tree.

Merry Christmas to all and blessings for a wonderful new year.

May your holidays ring with joy and good cheer!

Ring those Christmas bells.

Enjoy the magic of the holiday.

As you celebrate the season, may your home be filled with peace and joy.

In the stillness of this holy night, may Christ's peace be with you.

Ho! Ho! Ho!

Hoping your holidays are filled with the warmth and smiles of family and friends.

Christmas cookies and happy hearts,
That's the way the holiday starts.

What if Christmas doesn't come from a store? What if Christmas means a little bit more?

—the Grinch (Dr. Seuss)

Joy expressed, love shared, a miracle celebrated.

May all good things be yours this Christmas.

'Tis the season for shopping ... Hope your holidays are filled with laughter and fun.

Wishing you and the ones you love every blessing as we celebrate the season.

Hope Santa brings you a warm and wonderful Christmas.

In the wonder of this holy season, may you be truly blessed.

May the wonder and miracle of that holy night fill you with God's glorious love.

May your holidays be merry, and your new year filled with fun.

Wishing you sweet treats and all good things in this joyous holiday season.

Have yourself a merry little Christmas.

Believe in the magic of the season.

Mix, mingle and be merry.

A loving wish that holiday memories shine in your heart all year long.

Wishing you a joyous holiday season,
and peace and happiness in the new year.

May you be surrounded by friends, family and fun in this happy season.

May peace and joy light your way through the holidays.

Wishing you and yours a jolly holly day.

I'm dreaming of a white Christmas.

Sharing our season together.

Unto us a child is born.

May the blessings of Christmas bring you peace throughout the year.

Silent night, holy night.

Dear Santa,
I want it all!

May the love and peace of this joyous season surround you throughout the year.

May you be greatly blessed by God's love and grace in this holy season.

O Holy Night!

May the love of friends and family warm your heart and home.

Have you been naughty or nice?

Jesus is the reason for the season.

May the joys of this blessed season be with you throughout the New Year.

Encouragement

You must do the thing
you think you can not do!
-ELEANOR ROOSEVELT-

These are the days.

There are always more choices than you think.

—Catherine DeVrye

Don't let your
past dictate who
you are now,
but let it be part
of who you
will become.

Imagination
is the highest
kite one can fly.

—Lauren Bacall

Creativity takes courage.

—Henri Matisse

When it is dark enough, you can see the stars.

—Ralph Waldo Emerson

Believe the impossible.

Blessed are the happiness makers.

Things work out best for people who make
the best of the way things work out.

—John Wooden

Encouragement

Whatever you are, be a good one.

—Abraham Lincoln

We must be willing to get rid of the life we've planned, so as to have the life that is waiting for us.

—Joseph Campbell

Believe in miracles.

It's kind of fun to do the impossible.

—Walt Disney

Hope is putting faith to work when doubting would be easier.

Oh, my friend, it's not what they take away from you that counts. It's what you do with what you have left.

—Hubert Humphrey

Rock bottom is good solid ground, and a dead-end street is just a place to turn around.

—Buddy Buie and J.R. Cobb

Don't be afraid to take a big step if one is indicated; you can't cross a chasm in two small jumps.

—David Lloyd George

Try not to become a man of success, but rather try to become a man of value.

—Albert Einstein

It's what's inside that counts.

Kind words can be short and easy to speak, but their echoes are truly endless.

—Mother Teresa

Dance to the music of your dreams; the steps will bring you joy.

If you're going through hell, keep going.

—Winston Churchill

Out of difficulties grow miracles.

—Jean De La Bruyere

Life is the art of drawing without an eraser.

—John Gardner

Encouragement

We ourselves feel that what we are doing is just a drop in an ocean. But the ocean would be less because of that missing drop. —Mother Teresa

Life can only be understood backward, but it must be lived forward.
—Søren Kierkegaard

Hope is the thing with feathers that perches in the soul and sings the tune without the words and never stops ... at all.
—Emily Dickinson

Life is either a daring adventure or nothing.
—Helen Keller

It just wouldn't be a picnic without the ants.

Keep your heart in a place where dreams can grow.

The greatest mistake you can make in life is to be continually fearful that you will make one.

—Ellen Hubbard

Perhaps this very instant is your time.

—Louis Bogan

You're never as good as everyone tells you when you win, and you're never as bad as they say when you lose.

—Lou Holtz

Dream in color.

When the going gets tough, there's nothing like a good friend and a gallon of ice cream to lean on.

The grand essentials of happiness are something to do, something to love and something to hope for.

—A. R. Chalmers

No one is useless in this world who lightens the burdens of another.

—Charles Dickens

The journey between what you once were and who you are now becoming is where the dance of life really takes place. —Barbara De Angelis

Encouragement

Enjoy the little things, for one day you may look back and realize they were the big things.

—Robert Brault

The winds of grace are always blowing, but it is ours to set the sails.

There's nothing wrong with getting knocked down, as long as you get right back up.

—Muhammad Ali

Let nothing dim the light that shines from within.

—Maya Angelou

In good times or bad, I'm there for you.

The day will happen whether or not you get up.

—John Ciardi

If you can dream it, you can become it.

Make your optimism come true.

Every day may not be good,
but there's something good in every day.

The mightiest works have been accomplished by men who have somehow kept their ability to dream great dreams.

—Walter Russell Bowie

There's a light at the end of the tunnel.

What a day for a daydream.

The darkest hour has only 60 minutes.

—Morris Mandel

Whether it is the best of times or the worst of times, it is the only time you've got.

—Art Buchwald

You gain strength, courage and confidence by every experience in which you really stop to look fear in the face … you must do the thing you can not do.

—Eleanor Roosevelt

*E*ncouragement

If all the world's a stage, I want better lighting.

Wherever you go, no matter what the weather, always bring your own sunshine.

—Anthony J. D'Angelo

Find joy in the little things.

To dream of the person you would be is to waste the person you are.

You miss 100 percent of the shots you don't take.

Reach for the stars!

Just wanted you to know you're in my thoughts today.

When late morning rolls around, and you're feeling a bit out of sorts, don't worry; you're probably just a little 11 o'clockish.

—Winnie the Pooh (A.A. Milne)

Each day has its own purpose and fits into the great plan of our life.

—Carol Adrienne

If everything seems under control, you're just not going fast enough.

—Mario Andretti

Follow not in the footsteps of the masters, but rather seek what they sought.

Personality can open doors, but only character can keep them open.

Tomorrow is always fresh, with no mistakes in it.

—Lucy Maud Montgomery

Don't look back unless you plan to go back that way.

The future belongs to those who believe in the beauty of their dreams.

The greatest gift of all is to believe.

Encouragement

This is your day to shine.

We cannot direct the wind,
but we can adjust the sails.

You give me reason to believe.

A problem is a chance for you to do your best.

—Duke Ellington

Turn your face to the sun, and the shadows fall behind you.

—William Purkey

*I don't think
of all the misery,
but of the beauty
that still remains.*

—Anne Frank

Obstacles are those
frightful things
you see when you
take your eyes
off your goal.

—Henry Ford

Being defeated is often a temporary condition.

Giving up is what makes it permanent.

—Marilyn Vos Savant

"I tried, and it didn't work"
is a lot better than
"I wish I'd tried."

The time to be
happy is now.
The place to be
happy is here.

What's behind you doesn't matter.

—Enzo Ferrari

**If you travel a
path without
obstacles, it
probably doesn't
lead anywhere.**

—Catherine DeVrye

Only those who will
risk going too far
can possibly find out
how far one can go.

—T. S. Eliot

Promise me you will always
remember that you are braver
than you believe, and stronger
than you seem, and smarter
than you think.

—Winnie the Pooh (A.A. Milne)

*What if the
hokey pokey
really is what
it's all about?*

Fall seven times, stand up eight.

—Japanese proverb

You are a work of art.

Encouragement

Act as if what you do makes a difference. It does.
—William James

Don't be afraid to do something just because it's impossible.
—Kobi Yamada

Don't cry because it's over. Smile because it happened.
—Dr. Suess

Live in wonder.

Once you choose hope, anything's possible.
—Christopher Reeve

When you come to the end of your rope, tie a knot and hang on.
—Franklin D. Roosevelt

The purpose of our lives is to give birth to the best which is within us.
—Marianne Williamson

He who has a "why" to live can bear almost any "how."
—Friedrich Nietzsche

Giving up doesn't always mean you are weak. Sometimes it means that you are strong enough to let go.
—author unknown

I believe that every single event in life is an opportunity to choose love over fear. —Oprah Winfrey

All you need is deep within you waiting to unfold and reveal itself.

—Eileen Caddy

The future's so bright, you'd better wear shades!

Once we believe in ourselves, we can risk curiosity, wonder, spontaneous delight, or any experience that reveals the human spirit.

—e. e. cummings

The secret to having it all is believing that you already do.

Life is about becoming more than we are.

—Oprah Winfrey

You have to leave room in life to dream.

—Buffy Sainte-Marie

Eighty percent of success is showing up.

—Woody Allen

The family is one of life's masterpieces.

The family—that dear octopus from whose tentacles we never quite escape, nor in our inmost hearts, ever quite wish to.

—Dodie Smith

Always my brother, always my friend.

The family is a haven in a heartless world.

—Christopher Lasch

Other things may change us, but we start and end with the family.

—Anthony Brandt

Sisters are forever.

Loving family,
Mine to treasure,
Better than wealth
Of any measure.

No earthly joys could bring more pleasure than a little boy to love and treasure.

Family

Our family is a circle of strength and love. With every birth and every union, the circle grows. Every joy shared adds more love. Every crisis faced together makes the circle stronger.

Having someplace to go is home. Having someone to love is family. Having both ... is a blessing.

—author unknown

Happiness is having a large, loving, caring, close-knit family ... in another city.

—George Burns

A brother is someone you can lean on.

A family is one of life's special blessings.

Families are like fudge ... mostly sweet with a few nuts.

—author unknown

A daughter is the best friend you can have.

Families are a special blessing.

Families are tied together with heartstrings.

My sister ... my best friend.

FAMILY: A social unit where the father is concerned with parking space, the children with outer space, and the mother with closet space.

—Evan Esarr

I can't imagine in all the world a better brother than you.

I don't care how poor a man is; if he has family, he's rich.

—Thad Mumford and Dan Wilcox

Big sisters are the crabgrass in the lawn of life. —Charles M. Schulz

Give me a house to call my own, Family and friends to make it a home.

To have a daughter like you is to know a special kind of joy.

Family

*Always my daughter ...
now my friend.*

Blood's thicker than water, and when one's in trouble, best to seek out a relative's open arms. —author unknown

The informality of family life is a blessed condition that allows us to become our best while looking our worst.

—Marge Kennedy

There is no better friend than a brother.

Brothers are forever.

A cousin is a childhood playmate who grows into a forever friend.

If the family were a fruit, it would be an orange, a circle of sections, held together but separable—each segment distinct.

—Letty Cottin Pogrebin

A brother is
a friend forever.

**You don't choose
your family.
They are God's
gift to you, as
you are to them.**

—Desmond Tutu

When our relatives
are at home, we have
to think of all their
good points, or it
would be impossible
to endure them.

—George Bernard Shaw

A daughter
is a little girl
who grows up
to become a
wonderful friend.

Family is just accident. They don't mean to get on your nerves.
They don't even mean to be your family, they just are.

—Marsha Norman

Sisters are special friends.

A family is a circle of friends who love you.

*Family
is love.*

A son is such a joy.

Friendship

A friend lo... s 17:17
nd loves a... 7 A frien
es at all ti... end love

A friend loves
at all times.
Proverbs 17:17

Friend to friend.

I've had many friends with whom I've shared my time, but very few with whom I've shared my heart.

Girlfriend, you're amazing!

When I count my blessings, I count you twice!

I like the way you think!

It is more fun to talk with someone who doesn't use long, difficult words, but rather short, easy words like "What about lunch?" —Winnie the Pooh (A.A. Milne)

You make life sweet.

Together is the best place to be.

"Stay" is a charming word in a friend's vocabulary.

—Louisa May Alcott

Friendship

*Yes'm, old friends is always best,
'less you can catch a new one that's fit
to make an old one out of.*

—Sarah Orne Jewett

A friend loves at all times.

—Proverbs 17:17

Time may pass, and we may part, but true friends stay close at heart.

Choose your friends
like books ...
few but choice.

**Friendship
is made one
stitch at a time.**

As treasured
keepsakes
warm the
home, cherished
friendships
warm the heart.

Though one
wears fur and
the other feathers,
true friends
always stick
together.

The seasons may come and go, but friends last forever.

Piglet sidled up to Pooh from behind. "Pooh!" he whispered. "Yes, Piglet?" "Nothing," said Piglet, taking Pooh's paw. "I just wanted to be sure of you."

—A.A. Milne

Friendship is the thread that ties hearts together.

Life is a patchwork of friends.

There are many people that we meet in our lives, but only a few are worth getting to know.

You're one fine chick!

Our friendship is soda-licious.

I'm so glad that you are my friend.

It's the friends you can call up at 4 a.m. that matter.

—Marlene Dietrich

'Tis better by far at the rainbow's end
to find not gold but a true friend.

Friendship improves happiness and abates misery by doubling our joy and dividing our grief.

—Joseph Addison

A friend is someone who strengthens you with prayers, blesses you with love, and encourages you with hope.

Friends are flowers in the garden of life.

*Friendship lightens every burden
and makes the sun shine brighter.*

**Only your real friends will tell
you when your face is dirty.**

—Sicilian proverb

I'm celebrating today because you are my friend.

A single rose can be my garden ... a single friend, my world.

—Leo Buscaglia

Friendship makes every day a celebration of the heart.

Time passes; friendship stays right where it's put.

If friends were flowers, I'd pick you.

A friend like you makes a friend like me happy to have a friend like you.

A friend is someone who reaches for your hand and touches your heart.

Many people will walk into and out of your life, but only true friends will leave footprints in your heart.

—Eleanor Roosevelt

From one small seed of kindness, friendship grows.

A friend is a gift to treasure forever.

Good friends are never forgotten, they live within our hearts.

May our house always be too small to hold all of our friends.

Time and seasons change, but not the ways of friendship.

The best time to make friends is before you need them.

—Ethel Barrymore

If we should live to 103, best friends we shall then still be.

Lean on me.

The harmony between friends is sweeter than any choir.

You're absolutely fabulous—
no seriously, you are!

True friends grow separately without growing apart.

True friend.

Fishing for friends.

My dear friend.

I like you just the way you are.

A friend is one who knows you and loves you just the same.

—Ellen Hubbard

Old friends are the best friends.

Neighbors by chance,
friends by choice.

I can't imagine in all the world a better friend than you.

*Friends
are forever.*

A life truly blessed
is one encircled by
true friends.

Best friends listen to
what you don't say.

**When friends
are together,
hearts speak
without words.**

A real friend walks
in when the rest of
the world walks out.

Cherished friendships warm the heart.

Kindred Spirits.

Friends are the flowers
that bloom in life's garden.

A friend is someone who
accepts you just the way you are.

Friends are just a phone call away.

Friends are special.

Friends never drift apart.

Rain or shine, you're a friend of mine.

My best friend is the one who brings out the best in me.

—Henry Ford

There's no greater treasure than an old friend.

We need a good friend through the rough times.

The purr-fect friend.

Friends are like a pocket, everybody needs one.

A friend is a rare book of which but one copy is made.

A friend is one who opens
the door to home and heart.

A friend is the voice on
the other end of the line.

You're a wonderful reason to celebrate.

Through thick and thin.

A friend is someone
who listens with the heart.

Friends like you are few and far between.

**Whenever I think of you,
it makes me smile.**

Real friends listen with their heart.

Friends are the best collectibles.

A friend is a hug
for my heart.

**Sew nice to be
your friend.**

Good friends are forever.

Friends and flowers
make life a garden.

Love surrounds our friendship.

**Friendship is
a treasure.**

A friend like you is a
special hug from God.

Friendship
hits the spot.

*Friendship
blooms in
loving hearts.*

Our friendship
is tied with love.

Friend to friend, heart to heart.

Our friendship is sewn in love.

Special friends, special memories.

Friends are the patchwork of life.

Friends can always patch things up.

Our friendship is very special.

The road to a friend's house is never long.

A friend is always within reach.

A friend is someone who cares.

Friends are the sunshine of life.

Friendship starts in the heart.

Thoughts of you always make me smile.

A friend like you is a gift from God.

Friends to the very end.

Friends are joined heart to heart.

Friendship is a work of heart.

Everything is better with a friend.

The best antiques are old friends.

A true friend is the rarest of blessings.

A friend is someone you can lean on.

Gardens

plant a little sunshine.

plant
a
little

SUN
SHINE

Little by little, day by day, friends and flowers grow that way.

Often the prickly thorn produces tender roses.

—Ovid

Take time to smell the roses.

Perfumes are the feelings of flowers.

Dreams are the flowers that bloom in your heart.

Sow seeds of kindness.

Don't wear perfume in the garden— unless you want to be pollinated by bees.

—Anne Raver

Wherever you go, whatever you do, may your garden angel watch over you.

May all your weeds be wildflowers.

Plant a little
sunshine.

**May your day
be filled with
daisies.**

I think that if ever
a mortal heard
the voice of God,
it would be in a
garden at the cool
of the day.

—F. Frankfort Moore

God made
rainy days
so gardeners
could get the
housework done.

*And the day came when the risk it took
to remain tight inside the bud was more
painful than the risk it took to bloom.*

—Anais Nin

Thank you for being my sunshine every day.

Plant kindness, gather love.

You can bury a lot of troubles digging in the dirt.

Scatter seeds of happiness.
Sow seeds of kindness.

To be overcome by the fragrance of flowers is a delectable form of defeat.
—Beverly Nichols

A rose is a rose is a rose. —Gertrude Stein

It is utterly forbidden to be half-hearted about gardening. You have got to love your garden, whether you like it or not. —W.C. Sellar and R.J. Yeatman

The earth laughs in flowers.

Frogs are lucky, they can eat what bugs them.

Gardening requires lots of water— most of it in the form of perspiration.
—Lou Erickson

'Tis my faith that every flower enjoys the air it breathes!
—William Wordsworth

Don't be afraid to go out on a limb, that's where all the fruit is.

Gardening is a matter of your enthusiasm holding up until your back gets used to it.

—author unknown

Gardening is a kind of disease. It infects you; you cannot escape it. When you go visiting, your eyes rove about the garden; you interrupt serious cocktail drinking because of an irresistible impulse to get up and pull a weed.

—Lewis Gannit

A sprinkle of love makes friendship grow.

May your day be filled with roses.

Flowers say hello from the heart.

Nature does not hurry, yet everything is accomplished.

—Lao Tzu

Tiptoe through the tulips.

Bloom where you are planted.

April showers bring May flowers.

Let your heart bloom.

Those who plant kindness gather love.

Weather means more when you have a garden. There's nothing like listening to a shower and thinking how it is soaking in around your green beans. —Marcelene Cox

I appreciate the misunderstanding I have had with Nature over my perennial border. I think it is a flower garden; she thinks it is a meadow lacking grass, and tries to correct the error.

—Sara Stein

May your day be filled with sunflowers.

The kiss of the sun for pardon, the song of the birds for mirth; one is nearer God's heart in a garden, than anywhere else on earth. —Dorothy Francis Gurney

Get Well

Sorry you're not feeling well

A hug in a letter to make you feel better.

If you resolve to give up smoking,
drinking and loving,
you don't actually live longer;
it just seems longer.

—Clement Freud

Hoping you're up and about soon!

Happiness is your dentist
telling you it won't hurt,
and then having him
catch his hand in the drill.

—Johnny Carson

Sending you
healing wishes for
restful hours to
bring wellness to
each new day.

Udderly exhausted?

There must be
quite a few things
that a hot bath
won't cure, but I
don't know many
of them.

—Sylvia Plath, *The Bell Jar*

If wishes could make you well, you'd be better already.

I reckon being ill as one of the great pleasures of life, provided one is not too ill and is not obliged to work until one is better.

—Samuel Butler

Sending good cheer and plenty of good wishes to brighten your day!

Here's a cup of sunshine just for you.

I drive way too fast to worry about cholesterol.

Get well soon ... doctor's orders!

Life expectancy would grow by leaps and bounds if green vegetables smelled as good as bacon.

—Doug Larson

The greatest healing therapy is friendship and love.

—Hubert Humphrey

It's not the same without you. Get well soon!

I am pretty sure that, if you will be quite honest, you will admit that a good rousing sneeze, one that tears open your collar and throws your hair into your eyes, is really one of life's sensational pleasures.

—Robert Benchley

May God's love and care comfort you every day.

Warning: Humor may be hazardous to your illness.

—Ellie Katz

Sometimes I get the feeling the aspirin companies are sponsoring my headaches.

—V.L. Allineare

Sending smiles and sunshine and prayers your way and hoping you feel better soon!

The most important thing in illness is never to lose heart.

—Ellie Katz

Red meat is not bad for you. Now blue-green meat, that's bad for you!

—Tommy Smothers

Get Well

Sending you caring thoughts.

If I'd known I was going to live so long, I'd have taken better care of myself.

—Leon Eldred

May you find rest
in God's faithfulness,
find strength
in His promises
and be comforted
by His love as you
get well.

A good laugh and a long sleep are the best cures in the doctor's book.

—Irish Proverb

Are ewe doing OK?

Sending wishes
that you'll
feel better soon.

If you do everything you should do, and do not do anything you should not do, you will, according to the best available statistics, live exactly 18 hours longer than you would otherwise.

—Logan Clendening

Wishing you sunshine, daisies and brighter days ahead.

As you rest and heal, know that you are thought of warmly and wished a quick recovery.

Sorry you're not feeling well.

My own prescription for health is less paperwork and more running barefoot through the grass.

—Leslie Grimutter

Sending cheerful thoughts to brighten your day.

Hope you feel better soon.

If I had my way I'd make health catching instead of disease.

—Robert Ingersoll

The cure for anything is salt water—sweat, tears or the sea.

—Isak Dinesen

Sunny thoughts to brighten your day!

Holidays

May your troubles be less and
your blessings be more,
and nothing but happiness
come through your door.

Enjoy the delights of December,
and the hope of a new year.

Be always at war with your vices,
at peace with your neighbors, and let
each new year find you a better man.

—Benjamin Franklin

All bundled up for a warm holiday season.

May peace and happiness be yours
throughout this sacred season.

A New Year's resolution is something that goes in one year and out the other.

May this new year be the best ever!

People are so worried about what they eat between Christmas and the New Year, but they really should be worried about what they eat between the New Year and Christmas.

Cheers to a new year and another chance for us to get it right.

—Oprah Winfrey

Many people look forward to the new year for a new start on old habits.

Yesterday, everybody smoked his last cigar, took his last drink, and swore his last oath. Today, we are a pious and exemplary community. Thirty days from now, we shall have cast our reformation to the winds and gone to cutting our ancient shortcomings considerably shorter than ever.

—Mark Twain

Joyous holidays start with loving hearts and a happy home.

May all your troubles last as long as your New Year's resolutions.

—Joey Adams

One resolution I have made, and try to always keep, is this: to rise above the little things.

—John Burroughs

A best friend is like a four-leaf clover: hard to find and lucky to have.

May the magic of the Emerald Isle weave its charm all day long!

If you're enough lucky to be Irish, you're lucky enough! —Irish Saying

Blarney spoken here.

Feeling lucky.

May your troubles be less and your blessings be more, and nothing but happiness come through your door.

May your pockets
be heavy and your
heart be light,
May good luck
pursue you each
morning and night.

—Irish blessing

The luck of the Irish.

Never iron a four-leaf clover, because you don't want to press your luck.

Top of the morning.

Hippity-hopping down the bunny trail

to wish you a happy Easter.

Jelly beans, colored eggs and a chocolate bunny,

Here's hoping that your Easter day is very sweet and sunny!

Easter tells us that life is to be interpreted not simply in terms of things, but in terms of ideals.

—Charles M. Crowe

Have a candy-egg Easter and a jelly-bean spring!

Easter says you can put truth in a grave, but it won't stay there. —Clarence W. Hall

Easter blessings.

Have an egg-stra special day!

America, you're beautiful.

In the truest sense, freedom cannot be bestowed; it must be achieved. —Franklin D. Roosevelt

Freedom is nothing but a chance to be better.

—Albert Camus

Land of the free and home of the brave.

Freedom isn't free.

Let freedom never perish in your hands.

—Joseph Addison

What is the essence of America? Finding and maintaining that perfect, delicate balance between freedom "to" and freedom "from."

—Marilyn vos Savant

Liberty is always dangerous, but it is the safest thing we have.

—Harry Emerson Fosdick

God Bless America!

There is nothing wrong with America
that cannot be cured by what is right with America.

—William J. Clinton

From every mountainside
Let Freedom ring.

—Samuel F. Smith, *America*

Our hearts where they rocked our cradle,

Our love where we spent our toil,

And our faith, and our hope, and our honor,

We pledge to our native soil.

Where liberty dwells, there is my country.

—Benjamin Franklin

God gave all men all earth to love,

But since our hearts are small,

Ordained for each one spot should prove.

Beloved over all.

—Rudyard Kipling

We must be free not because we claim freedom, but because we practice it.

—William Faulkner

It is easy to take liberty for granted,
when you have never had it taken from you.

—Dick Cheney

United we stand.

Liberty means
responsibility.
That is why most
men dread it.

—George Bernard Shaw

**This nation
will remain the
land of the free
only so long as it
is the home
of the brave.**

—Elmer Davis

May the sun in his course
visit no land more free,
more happy, more lovely,
than this our own country!

—Daniel Webster

This land is your land.

Land that I love.

Sweet land of liberty.

*Patriotism ... is not short, frenzied outbursts of emotion,
but the tranquil and steady dedication of a lifetime.*

—Adlai Stevenson

Best witches and happy haunting.

Once in a young lifetime one should be allowed to have as much sweetness as one can possibly want and hold.

—Judith Olney

"Boo" from the crew.

Eat, drink and be scary.

I'll bet living in a nudist colony takes all the fun out of Halloween.

A spooky "boo" day to you.

There's nothing on Earth so beautiful as the final haul on Halloween night.

—Steve Almond

Blood donors needed ... see the Count.

Best witches of the season.

Happy Halloween.

Bone Voyage.

Happy Haunting.

Pumpkins for sale.

Bootiful.

Best witches.

From ghoulies
and ghosties,

And long-leggedy beasties,

And things that go
bump in the night,

Good Lord, deliver us!

—Scottish saying

On Halloween the thing you must do,
Is pretend that nothing can frighten you,
And if somethin' scares you, and you want to run,
Just let on like it's Halloween fun.

Boo to you!

At this time of counting blessings, you always come to mind.

God gave you a gift of 86,400 seconds today. Have you used one to say "thank you?"

—William A. Ward

To speak gratitude is courteous and pleasant; to enact gratitude is generous and noble; but to live gratitude is to touch Heaven.

—Johannes A. Gaertner

Caution: turkey crossing.

On Thanksgiving Day we acknowledge our dependence.

—William Jennings Bryan

Be thankful.

An optimist is a person who starts a new diet on Thanksgiving Day.

—Irv Kupcinet

On Thanksgiving Day, all over America, families sit down to dinner at the same moment—halftime.

Gratitude is happiness doubled by wonder.

Gather a harvest of love.

We gather together to ask the Lord's blessing.

Thanksgiving is an emotional holiday. People travel thousands of miles to be with people they only see once a year. And then discover once a year is way too often.

—Johnny Carson

We can only be said to be alive in those moments when our hearts are conscious of our treasures.

—Thornton Wilder

We give thanks for unknown blessings already on their way.

Hem your blessings with thankfulness so they don't unravel.

—author unknown

Coexistence: what the farmer does with the turkey until Thanksgiving.

—Mike Connolly

Thanksgiving dinners take 18 hours to prepare. They are consumed in 12 minutes. Halftimes take 12 minutes. This is not coincidence.

—Erma Bombeck

Nothing is more honorable than a grateful heart. —Seneca

Happy Thanksgiving.

Thanksgiving was never meant to be shut up in a single day.
—Robert Caspar Lintner

Turkey: a large bird whose flesh, when eaten on certain religious anniversaries, has the peculiar property of attesting piety and gratitude.
—Ambrose Bierce

Thanksgiving, after all, is a word of action.
—W.J. Cameron

Bountiful blessings.

Thanksgiving is possible only for those who take time to remember; no one can give thanks who has a short memory.
—author unknown

For each new morning with its light,
For rest and shelter of the night,
For health and food, for love and friends,
For everything Thy goodness sends.

—Ralph Waldo Emerson

May your stuffing be tasty,
May your turkey be plump,
May your potatoes and gravy,
Have nary a lump.
May your yams be delicious,
And your pies take the prize,
And may your Thanksgiving dinner,
Stay off of your thighs!

Let's talk turkey.

As we express our gratitude,
we must never forget that the
highest appreciation is not to
utter words, but to live by them.

—John Fitzgerald Kennedy

Happy Turkey Day.

Perhaps it takes a purer faith to praise God for unrealized blessings
than for those we once enjoyed, or those we enjoy now.

—A.W. Tozer

Harvest greetings.

Be ye thankful.

*Thanksgiving Day comes, by statute, once a year; to the honest
man it comes as frequently as the heart of gratitude will allow.*

—Edward Sandford Martin

Hand over the **CHOCOLATE** and no one will get hurt!!!

You win some, you lose some, you wreck some.
—Dale Earnhardt

I am woman! I am invincible! I am pooped!
—author unknown

My memory is remarkable ... I forget everything.

Blessed are they who can laugh at themselves, for they shall never cease to be amused.

You're a good egg, just a little cracked.

The first rule of holes: When you're in one, stop digging.
—Molly Ivins

When in doubt, take a nap.

The problem with people who have no vices is that generally you can be pretty sure they're going to have some pretty annoying virtues. —Elizabeth Taylor

Who needs a man? If it's heartache you want, let's go try on bikinis!

The statistics on sanity show that one out of every four Americans is suffering from some form of mental illness. Think of your three best friends. If they're okay, then it's you.

—Rita Mae Brown

Time may be a great healer, but it's a lousy beautician.

If at first you don't succeed, find out if the loser gets anything.

—Bill Lyon

Normal is nothing more than a cycle on a washing machine.

—Whoopi Goldberg

They say that nobody is perfect. Then they say practice makes perfect. I wish they'd make up their minds.

—Phyllis Diller

I'm tired, and I want a cookie.

My family tree is full of nuts.

Man cannot live on chocolate alone, but women can.

Some people feel rain, others just get wet.

You're only as good as your last haircut.

—Fran Lebowitz

Every oak tree started out as a couple of nuts
who decided to stand their ground.

—author unknown

**A positive
attitude may
not solve all
your problems,
but it will annoy
enough people
to make it worth
the effort.**

—Herm Albright

If the world
were a logical place,
men would ride
sidesaddle.

—Rita Mae Brown

Cherish yesterday,
dream tomorrow,
live like crazy today.

Forget love ... I'd rather fall in chocolate!

All you really need is a rad set of wheels and some cool cats to hang out with.

I breathe, therefore I shop.

There is no life before coffee.

I asked for a Mustang for my birthday.

I should have been more specific.

Housework can't kill you, but why take a chance.

—Phyllis Diller

Life is not orderly. No matter how we try to make life so, right in the middle of it we die, lose a leg, fall in love, drop a jar of applesauce. —Natalie Goldberg

Reality is the leading cause of stress among those in touch with it.

—Lily Tomlin

I don't do mornings.

It's never too late in fiction or in life to revise.

—Nancy Thayer

Mirror, mirror on the wall, I'm like my mother after all.

If not for chocolate, there would be no need for control-top pantyhose. An entire garment industry would be devastated.

—author unknown

Advice is what we ask for when we already know the answer but wish we didn't.

—Erica Jong

A bad day at golf is better than a good day at work.

Wrinkles merely indicate where smiles have been.

It's always something.

—Gilda Radner as Rosanne Rosannadanna

Give me chocolate, and no one gets hurt.

Love

I love thee to the depth and breadth and height my soul can reach.
ELIZABETH BARRETT BROWNING

You make my world a beautiful place to live and grow.

The secret of a happy marriage remains a secret.
—Henny Youngman

Always: every minute of every day.

My life is so blessed because you are in it.

Live fully. Laugh often. Love deeply.

Happiness is being with you.

Sealed with a kiss.

The bonds of matrimony are like any other bonds—they mature slowly.
—Peter De Vries

SPOUSE: someone who'll stand by you through all the trouble you wouldn't have had if you'd stayed single.

Love

Always kiss me good night.

Now these three remain:
faith, hope and love.
But the greatest of these is love.

—1 Corinthians 13:13

The best thing to hold onto in life is each other.

True love begins
when nothing
is looked for in return.

—Antoine de Saint-Exupéry

**You remind
me of the sun,
you brighten
my day.**

The best and most
beautiful things
in the world cannot
be seen or even
touched ... they must
be felt with the heart.

—author unknown

In true love, the
smallest distance is
too great, and the
greatest distance
can be bridged.

—Hans Nouwens

Whatever our souls are made of, his and mine are the same.

—Emily Bronte

An anniversary is a time to celebrate the joys of today, the memories of yesterday, and the hopes of tomorrow.

To truly love someone, we must laugh with them.

I love the person you are.

What a grand thing to be loved. What a grander thing to love.

—Victor Hugo

Never go to bed mad. Stay up and fight.

—Phyllis Diller

BLISS: total happiness; joy; the feeling that nothing is more perfect than this moment.

May the God of love be the heart of your marriage, the light of your home, and the ever-present partner in your new life together.

An archaeologist is the best husband a woman can have. The older she gets the more interested he is in her.

—Agatha Christie

It's so great to find that one special person you want to annoy for the rest of your life.

—Rita Rudner

In all you dream and all you do, may the love you share bring joy to you.

How do I love thee? Let me count the ways.

—Elizabeth Barrett Browning

I made a wish, and you came true!

If love is blind, why is lingerie so popular?

For you see, each day I love you more—today more than yesterday and less than tomorrow.

—Rosemonde Gerard

Love is a fruit in season at all times, and within reach of every hand.

—Mother Teresa

You hold the key to my heart.

I love thee to the depth and breadth and height my soul can reach.

—Elizabeth Barrett Browning

ADORE: to regard with devotion and love; to feel a deep attachment.

We are all a little weird, and life's a little weird, and when we find someone whose weirdness is compatible with ours, we join up with them and fall in mutual weirdness and call it love.

—author unknown

Love and laughter, Happily ever after.

 *Love*

Be mine!

Two hearts to cherish.
One life to share.

Where there is great love, there are always miracles.

—Willa Cather

Love is not a matter of counting the years,

it's a matter of making the years count.

—Theophrastus

Love is a song the heart sings … what a beautiful song you sing.

Those who wish to sing always find a song … you help me hear the music.

Eternal Love

Chains do not hold a marriage together. It is threads, hundreds of tiny threads which sew people together through the years.

—Simone Signoret

Sharing our joy together.

The essence of love is kindness.

—Robert Louis Stevenson

Success in marriage does not come merely through finding the right mate, but through being the right mate.

—Barnett R. Brickner

When I followed my heart, it led right to you.

Happy is my heart because you said you'd be mine!

Wishing two people one wonderful life.

Happiness is being married to your best friend.

A journey is like marriage. The certain way to be wrong is to think you control it.

—John Steinbeck

Our love is the greatest gift we can give each other.

Love is like the measles. The older you get it, the worse the attack.

—Mary Roberts Rhinehart

Love

There are souls
in this world who have
the gift of finding
joy everywhere and
of leaving it behind
them when they go.

—Frederick Faber

Heaven bless your
togetherness.

**Wishing you
love and
laughter
forever after.**

Our wedding was
many years ago.
The celebration
continues to
this day.

—Gene Perret

Fairy tales do come true.

Who so loves,
believes the impossible.

—Elizabeth Barrett Browning

Falling in love consists merely in uncorking
the imagination and bottling the common sense.

—Helen Rowland

Sharing sweet moments together.

A wedding anniversary is the celebration of love,
trust, partnership, tolerance and tenacity.
The order varies for any given year.

—Paul Sweeney

Some people come into our lives and leave footprints on our hearts, and we are never the same.

—Flavia Weedn

You're my inspiration.

**'Twas not
my lips
you kissed,
but my soul.**

—Judy Garland

Love one another, and
you will be happy.
It's as simple and as
difficult as that.

—Michael Leunig

A successful
marriage requires
falling in love many
times, always with
the same person.

—Mignon McLaughlin

Music is love
in search of a word.

Miscellaneous

Hoping your day is PURR-FECT!

Music is said to be the speech of angels.

A star for luck, an angel for guidance.

I've seen and met angels wearing the disguise of ordinary people living ordinary lives.

—Tracy Chapman

Don't run faster than your guardian angel can fly.

I am sending an angel ahead of you to guard you along the way.

Wherever you go and whatever you do,
May your guardian angel watch over you.

An angel in the house, they say,
Will guard your family night and day.

An angel in the kitchen, watching the stew,
Blesses your cooking and all that you do.

Miscellaneous

By working faithfully eight hours a day, you may eventually get to be boss and work 12 hours a day.

—Robert Frost

No one who achieves success does so without acknowledging the help of others. The wise and confident acknowledge this help with gratitude.

—author unknown

No one is more cherished in this world than someone who lightens the burden of another. Thank you.

—author unknown

One measure of leadership is the caliber of people who choose to follow you.

—Dennis A. Peer

If a train station is where the train stops, what's a work station? —author unknown

Accomplishing the impossible means only that the boss will add it to your regular duties.

—Doug Larson

A teacher sees tomorrow in a child's eye.

Old postal employees never die; they just lose their zip.

Nursing is a work of the heart.

Volunteers do not necessarily have the time; they just have the heart.

—Elizabeth Andrew

Hairstylists are a cut above the rest.

Teachers have class.

I think of a hero as someone who understands the degree of responsibility that comes with his freedom.

—Bob Dylan

The hero is commonly the simplest and obscurest of men.

—Henry David Thoreau

Anyone can drive a car, but it takes someone special to drive a bus.

A teacher's task: to take a lot of live wires and make sure they're well-grounded.

Miscellaneous

How important it is for us to recognize and celebrate our heroes and she-roes!

—Maya Angelou

Leaders need to be optimists. Their vision is beyond the present.

—Rudy Giuliani

Firefighters save hearts and homes.

—author unknown

Nurses have patience.

The world is hugged by the faithful arms of volunteers.

—Everett Mámor

Sometimes angels are disguised as teachers.

Creative types are seldom tidy.

To teach is to touch a life forever.

Leaders are visionaries with a poorly developed sense of fear and no concept of the odds against them.

—Robert Jarvic

Dogs are not our whole life,
but they make our life whole.

—Roger Caras

In order to keep a true perspective of one's importance, everyone should have a dog that will worship him, and a cat that will ignore him.

—Dereke Bruce

If cats could talk, they wouldn't.

—Nan Porter

One reason
a dog can be such
a comfort when
you're feeling blue
is that he doesn't
try to find out why.

The more I see of
man, the more
I like dogs.

—Mme de Staël

Hoping
your day
is purr-fect.

A man may smile and bid you hail,
Yet wish you to the devil;
But when a good dog wags his tail,
You know he's on the level.

Miscellaneous

Some people say that cats are sneaky, evil, and cruel. True, and they have many other fine qualities as well.

—Missy Dizick

The man who carries a cat by the tail learns something that can be learned in no other way.

—Mark Twain

In ancient times cats were worshipped as gods; they have not forgotten this.

—Terry Pratchett

It is impossible to keep a straight face in the presence of one or more kittens.

—Cynthia E. Varnado

Anybody who doesn't know what soap tastes like has never washed a dog.

—Faith Resnick

People that hate cats will come back as mice in their next life.

—Faith Resnick

Meow is like aloha—it can mean anything.

—Hank Ketchum

Dogs have owners, cats have staff.

If you get to thinking you're a person of some influence, try ordering somebody else's dog around.

—Will Rogers

One must love a cat on its own terms.

—Paul Gray

People who love cats have some of the biggest hearts around.

To err is human, to purr is feline.

—Robert Byrne

Dogs come when they're called; cats take a message and get back to you later. —Mary Bly

As every cat owner knows, nobody owns a cat.

—Ellen Perry Berkeley

The reason cats climb is so that they can look down on almost every other animal—it's also the reason they hate birds.

—K.C. Buffington

Occasions

Wishing you a new world to conquer and new adventures to discover.

Congratulations!

All of our dreams can come true, if we have the courage to pursue them.

—Walt Disney

Learning is a treasure that will follow its owner everywhere.

—Chinese Proverb

One can never consent to creep when one feels an impulse to soar.

—Helen Keller

Education is not preparation for life; education is life itself.

—John Dewey

Just about a month from now I'm set adrift, with a diploma for a sail and lots of nerve for oars.

—Richard Halliburton

If you make the world a little better, then you have accomplished a great deal.

—author unknown

Commencement speeches were invented largely in the belief that outgoing college students should never be released into the world until they have been properly sedated.

—Garry Trudeau

The ornaments of your house will be the guests who frequent it.

May the roof above us never fall in, and may we good companions beneath it never fall out.

—Irish Blessing

The universe is merely a fleeting idea in God's mind—a pretty uncomfortable thought, particularly if you've just made a down payment on a house.

—Woody Allen

May love and happiness surround you in your new home.

Hospitality is making your guests feel at home—even if you wish they were.

May love surround your new home.

There's nothing to match curling up with a good book when there's a repair job to be done around the house.

—Joe Ryan

I always thought a yard was three feet, then I started mowing the lawn.
—C.E. Cowman

May your new home be filled with the joys of friends and family.

A home is a house with a heart inside.

Where we love is home—home that
our feet may leave, but not our hearts.
—Oliver Wendell Holmes Sr.

One only needs two tools in life: WD-40 to make things go, and duct tape to make them stop.
—G.M. Weilacher

May your new home be blessed with peace and joy, much love, good health and prosperity.

Wishing you every happiness in your new home.

A house is built with boards and beams; a home is built with love and dreams.

Dance as if no one were watching, sing as if no one were listening, and live every day as if it were your last.

—Irish proverb

Life consists not in holding good cards, but in playing those you hold well. —Josh Billing

I wish to live because life has with it that which is good and that which is beautiful and that which is love.

—author unknown

Life moves pretty fast. If you don't stop and look around once in a while, you could miss it.

—Ferris Bueller

Wishing you a new world to conquer and new adventures to discover.

Simple pleasures are best.

Vacation: having nothing to do and all day to do it.

All the art of living lies in a fine mingling of letting go and holding on.

—Henry Ellis

May you live all the days of your life.

Some people come into our lives and leave footprints
on our hearts, and we are never the same.

—Flavia Weedn

It is not the length of life, but the depth of life!

—Ralph Waldo Emerson

Life's a dance
you learn as you go.

Life is a daring adventure
or nothing at all.

—Helen Keller

**Be glad of life,
because it gives
you the chance
to love and to
play and to look
at the stars.**

I still find each day
too short for all the
thoughts I want to think,
all the walks I want to
take, all the books I
want to read, and all the
friends I want to see.

—John Burroughs

Occasions

Hope everything's going well in your corner of the world!

What is the opposite of two? A lonely me, a lonely you.

—Richard Wilbur

Sometimes, when one person is missing, the whole world seems depopulated.

—Lamartine

Always on my mind, forever in my heart.

I wouldn't mind being lonely if you were there to keep me company.

May the road rise up to meet you, may the wind be ever at your back. May the sun shine warm upon your face and the rain fall softly on your fields. And until we meet again, may God hold you in the hollow of his hand.

—Irish Blessing

The reason it hurts so much to separate is because our souls are connected.

—Nicholas Sparks, *The Notebook*

The world is round, and the place which may seem like the end may also be only the beginning.

—Ivy Baker Priest

I dropped a tear in the ocean; the day you find it is the day I will stop missing you.

—author unknown

I think about you constantly, whether it's with my mind or my heart.

—Albany Bach Reid

Journey: an experience or process that leaves you changed.

Wishing you calm seas and a gentle breeze!

The one good thing about not seeing you is that I can write you letters.

—Svetlana Alliluyeva Sr.

Waddle I do without you?

I've been attending lots of seminars in my retirement. They're called naps. —Merri Brownworth

A retired husband is often a wife's full-time job.

—Ella Harris

The money's no better in retirement, but the hours are!

Retirement is a fishing trip that never ends.

Enjoy new adventures!

The challenge of retirement is how to spend time without spending money.

Retirement: It's nice to get out of the rat race, but you have to learn to get along with less cheese.

—Gene Perret

Golf is played by 20 million mature American men whose wives think they are out having fun.

—Jim Bishop

I'm retired—goodbye tension, hello pension!

The trouble with retirement is that you never get a day off.

—Abe Lemons

The best time to start thinking about your retirement is before the boss does.

Don't underestimate the value of Doing Nothing, of just going along, listening to all the things you can't hear, and not bothering.

—*Pooh's Little Instruction Book*, inspired by A.A. Milne

Retirement kills more people than hard work ever did.

—Malcolm Forbes

Retirement is a golf vacation that never ends.

I'm not just retiring from the company, I'm also retiring from my stress, my commute, my alarm clock and my iron.

—Hartman Jule

Retirement: world's longest coffee break.

Parenting

Thinking of you, especially today and wishing you a Happy Father's Day!

Mothers are special blessings.

A mother is someone who can take the place of all others, but whose place no one else can take.

The only thing better than having you for my mother, is my children having you for their grandmother.

Parenting: results may vary.

Mother love is the fuel that enables a normal human being to do the impossible.

—Marion C. Garretty

There's a special place in heaven for the mother of boys.

I picked a very special mom.

No matter how calmly you try to referee, parenting will eventually produce bizarre behavior, and I'm not talking about the kids.

—Bill Cosby

Mom—I want
to be just like you!

I remembered my
mother's prayers,
and they have
always followed me.
They have clung to
me all my life.

—Abraham Lincoln

More than merely a mother ... slightly less than God.

We laugh, we cry,
We make time fly,
Best friends are we,
My mom and I.

*My mother taught me to think ahead ...
"If you don't pass your spelling test,
you'll never get a good job!"*

I know how to do anything—I'm a mom.

—Roseanne Barr

M is for Mom, not Maid.

Mothers of little boys work from son up 'til son down.

Parenthood: That state of being better chaperoned than you were before marriage.

—Marcelene Cox

God gave us memories so we could have roses in winter and mothers forever.

The sweetest sounds to mortals given are heard in Mother, Home and Heaven.

—William Goldsmith Brown

A mother is the best friend you can have.

Motherhood is like Albania—you can't trust the descriptions in the book, you have to go there. —Marni Jackson

If at first you don't succeed, do it like your mother told you.

—author unknown

MOTHER: a female parent; a woman with the capacity to give life and love to children.

The memories I treasure and hold most dear are of you, Mother.

Parents were invented to make children happy by giving them something to ignore.

—Ogden Nash

Mothers are special … especially mine.

Sometimes angels are disguised as mothers.

I smile because I am your mother. I laugh because you can't do anything about it.

Being a full-time mother is one of the highest salaried jobs in my field, since the payment is pure love.

—Mildred B. Vermont

The heart of a mother is a deep abyss, at the bottom of which you know you'll always find happiness.

—Honoré de Balzac

The art of mothering is to teach the art of living to children.

—Elain Heffner

Mothers and daughters become closer when daughters become mothers.

My mother taught me logic ... "If you fall off that swing and break your neck, you can't go to the store with me."

Mothers hold their children's hands for a while ... their hearts forever.

Joy overflows and sees us through,
In a home that is blessed by a mom like you.

A mother's arms are made of tenderness, and children sleep soundly in them. —Victor Hugo

Moms make memories

My mother taught me about receiving ... "You are going to get it when we get home."

Mother is another name for love.

My mother taught me ESP ... "Put your sweater on; don't you think I know when you're cold?"

A mother is someone you never outgrow.

What is a home without a mother?

—Nathaniel Hawthorne

The moment a child is born, the mother is also born. She never existed before. The woman existed, but the mother, never. A mother is something absolutely new.

—Bhaqwan Shree Rajneesh

Mothers are special angels.

I will not have a temper tantrum nor stomp across the floor,
I will not pout, scream or shout or kick against the door,
I will not throw my food around nor pick upon another,
I'll always try to be real good because I am the mother.

—author unknown

A father is one of life's special blessings.

Thank heaven for daddies.

It is not flesh
and blood,
but the heart
which makes us
fathers and sons.

—Johann Schiller

Oh, what a tangled web
do parents weave, when
they think that their
children are naive.

—Ogden Nash

I love my father as the
stars—he's a bright shining
example and a happy
twinkling in my heart.

—Adabella Radici

A father is someone you can lean on.

It is admirable for a man
to take his son fishing, but there is
a special place in heaven for the father
who takes his daughter shopping.

—John Sinor

A father like you is a gift from God.

We may not shower him with praise,
Nor mention his name in song,
And it seems that we forget the joy
He spreads as he goes along.
But it doesn't mean that we don't know
The wonderful role he has had.
And away down deep in every heart,
There's a place that is just for Dad.

—author unknown

The guys who fear becoming fathers don't understand that fathering is not something perfect men do, but something that perfects the man. The end product of child-raising is not the child but the parent.

—Frank Pittmannit

Thinking of you, especially today and wishing you a Happy Father's Day!

Fathers are special.

The best thing a father can do for his children is love their mother.

Happiness is having a dad like you.

A father is a man you look up to, no matter how tall you grow.

Hope your special day measures up!

There was never a great man who had not a great mother.
—Olive Schreiner

Dads are special, especially mine.

Dad knows best, but no one listens.

The quickest way for a parent to get a child's attention is to sit down and look comfortable.
—Lane Olinghouse

A truly rich man is one whose children run into his arms when his hands are empty.

A daddy is a man who has photos in his wallet where his money used to be.

Blessed indeed is the man who hears many gentle voices call him Father!
—Lydia M. Child

The best inheritance a father can leave his children is a good example.

*When my grandchildren say I rock,
they're not talking about a rocking chair.*

—Doris Roberts

Grandchildren are a gift from God.

The best antiques are grandparents.

*The trouble with being a parent is that by
the time you are experienced, you are unemployed.*

—author unknown

*Grandparents are
God's gift to children.*

Grandmas are moms
with lots of frosting.

—author unknown

Nobody can do for
little children what
grandparents do.
Grandparents sort of
sprinkle stardust over the
lives of little children.

—Alex Haley

**Grandma
knows best,
but no one
ever listens.**

Grandfathers are special.

The reason grandchildren and grandparents get along so well is that they have a common enemy.

—Sam Levenson

The simplest toy, one which even the youngest child can operate, is called a grandparent.

—Sam Levenson

Grandmothers are angels in training.

Grandmas are special angels.

Happiness is having grandchildren.

Grandmothers are a special blessing.

You do not really understand something unless you can explain it to your grandmother.

—Albert Einstein

Religious

Sending you a
little prayer...

...that God will keep
you in His care.

God will always give what is right to his people who cry to him night and day, and he will not be slow to answer them.

—Luke 18:7

The Lord is close to the brokenhearted, and he saves those whose Spirits have been crushed. —Psalms 34:18

In those times when I can't seem to find God, I rest in the reassurance that He knows how to find me.

—Neva Coyle

The Lord himself will go before you. He will be with you; he will not leave you or forget you.

—Deuteronomy 31:8

May God's love and care comfort you every day!

God keeps his promises.

God is hope. God is comfort. God is with you.

Religious

By day the Lord directs his love, at night his song is with me.

—Psalms 42:8

Don't fear tomorrow; God is already there.

My grace is enough for you. When you are weak, my power is made strong in you.

—2 Corinthians 12:9

Be strong in the Lord and in his great power.

—Ephesians 6:10

May guardian angels watch over you.

The Lord hears good people when they cry out to him, and he saves them from all their trouble.

—Psalms 34:17

Every sunrise is a gift from God.

We turn to God for help when our foundations are shaking, only to learn that it is God who is shaking them.

—Charles C. West

God is, and all is well. —John Whittier

The Lord is close to everyone who prays to him, to all who truly pray to him. —Psalms 145:18

The Lord bless you and keep you.

If God is for us, who can be against us? —Romans 8:31

God has made all things beautiful in his time.

You will know that God's power is very great for us who believe.
—Ephesians 1:19

Sending you a little prayer … that God will keep you in His care.

There's an angel watching over you in good times, trouble or stress. He wraps his wings 'round you, whispering, "You are loved and blessed."
—author unknown

When suffering comes, we yearn for some sign from God, forgetting we have just had one.

—Mignon McLaughlin

Come to me, all who are burdened, and I will give you rest.

—Matthew 11:28

I am sending an angel ahead of you to guard you along the way.

—author unknown

Pray and ask God for everything you need, always giving thanks.

—Philippians 4:6

Give all your worries to him, because he cares about you.

—1 Peter 5:7

Trust in the Lord with all your heart.

Depend on the Lord, trust in him, and he will take care of you. —Psalms 37:5

*Some of God's greatest gifts
are unanswered prayers.* —Garth Brooks

Wherever you go and whatever you do,
may your guardian angel watch over you.

With God all things are possible.

*Be joyful in hope,
patient in affliction, faithful in prayer.*

—Romans 12:12

May God give you ...
For every storm a rainbow,
For every tear a smile,
For every care a promise,
And a blessing in every trial.
For every problem life sends
A faithful friend to share,
For every sigh a sweet song
And an answer for each prayer.

—Irish blessing

God understands.

**Never will
I leave you,
never will
I forsake you.**

—Hebrews 13:5

Seasons

celebrate spring! Celeb
spring! Celeb ate spring
elebrate spr ng! Celeb

Promise of spring.

Dashing through the snow.

Summer afternoon—
summer afternoon;
to me those have always
been the two most
beautiful words in the
English language.

—Henry James

May the
bounty of the
season fill
your heart and
your home.

Cold hands, warm heart.

Snowflakes are one of nature's most fragile things, but just look at what they can do when they stick together.

—Vesta M. Kelly

Fun in the summer sun.

A fallen leaf is nothing more than a summer's wave goodbye.

I love snowy days, frosty nights and warm hearts.

Our Lord has written the promise of resurrection not in books alone, but in every leaf in springtime.

—Martin Luther

When life gives you snow, giggle!

The season has arrived. Enjoy all the good things it brings.

Winter is an etching,
spring a watercolor,
summer an oil painting,
and autumn
a mosaic of them all.

—Stanley Horowitz

May all the beauty of the season be yours throughout the year.

An optimist
is the human
personification
of spring.

—Susan J. Bissonette

Scarecrows, corn rows,
Pumpkins on the vine,
Leaves curl, wind swirls,
Fall is right on time.

SPRING: the season between winter and summer when plants and flowers begin to grow again; the time for sunshine and showers, planting and growing, bunnies and chicks.

Blossom by blossom, spring begins.

—Swinburne

Snowmen fall from heaven unassembled.

May all the joys of the season be yours.

Springtime is the land awakening.
The March winds are the morning yawn.

—Lewis Grizzard

Autumn greetings.

Wishing you all the joys of the season.

It was one of those March days when the sun shines hot and the wind blows cold; when it is summer in the light and winter in the shade.

—Charles Dickens

Ah, summer, what power you have
to make us suffer and like it.

—Russel Baker

Wishing you all the wonders of the season.

Snow friends come and go with seasons, but real friends last forever.

Love is to the heart what the summer is to the farmer's year — it brings to harvest all the loveliest flowers of the soul.

—author unknown

There shall be eternal summer in the grateful heart.

—Celia Thaxter

One kind word can warm three winter months.

—Japanese proverb

Spring is nature's way of saying, "Let's party!"

—Robin Williams

Through each passage and each season may you trust the goodness of life.

Every spring is the only spring, a perpetual astonishment.

—Ellis Peters

No winter lasts forever; no spring skips its turn.

—Hal Borland

Warm winter wishes.

It's difficult to think anything but pleasant thoughts while eating a homegrown tomato.

—Lewis Grizzard

Celebrate spring!

God gave us memory so that we might have roses in December.

—J.M. Barrie

The naked earth is warm with spring,

And with green grass and bursting trees

Leans to the sun's kiss glorying,

And quivers in the sunny breeze. —Julian Grenfell

sadness flies away on the wings of time

Sadness flies away on wings of time

God is hope, God is comfort,
God is with you.

May love comfort you at this difficult time.

Wishing you comfort and peace in this time of sorrow.

With all the beauties of seasons past,
look softly with the eyes of love and listen
with your heart ... your dear one will be there.

It's the spirit of a person that touches us, staying with us forevermore.

Our thoughts are with you
in this time of sadness.

Our prayers are with you
in this time of sorrow.

May time soften
the pain until
all that remains
is the beauty
of the memories
and the love,
always the love.

May nature touch you with compassion, bless you with sunlight and send gentle rain to quietly weep with you. May the breeze whisper life that never ends, only that it is changed—that it continues forever in a world more beautiful than our words can describe.

—author unknown

Earth has no sorrow that heaven cannot heal.

—Thomas Moore

Remembering your loved one as a very special person and sending you heartfelt sympathy.

May the Love of those around you help you through the days ahead.

With each tear that falls, may your spirit be renewed.

What the heart once owned and had, it shall never lose.

—Henry Ward Beecher

Thinking of you in your hour of sorrow and extending heartfelt sympathy.

Memories are the key not to the past, but to the future.
—Corrie Ten Boom

Her spirit will soar forever!
—Doris Mager, the Eagle Lady

You are in our thoughts and prayers.

Thanking God for your loved one's life and thinking of you during this difficult time.

We will remember the warm smile, the loving words, the caring heart … thinking of you during this time of loss.

With heartfelt sympathy.

May you find courage to face tomorrow in the love that surrounds you today.

There are no words to fill the emptiness in your heart … but perhaps it will help to know others care.

You know that you are not alone at this difficult time, and may you feel the comfort and friendship of those who share your loss.

May your sorrow be softened by the love that still unites you and by the cherished memories you will always carry in your heart.

May kind thoughts and cherished memories sustain you in your time of sorrow and bring you some measure of peace.

Praying for your comfort in this season of sadness.

May you find comfort in knowing our thoughts and prayers are with you.

May you find love all around you.

Sharing the sadness of your loss.

Sadness flies away on the wings of time.

May you find rest in God's faithfulness, find strength
in His promises and be comforted by His love.

Death leaves a heartache no one can heal,
Love leaves a memory no one can steal.

—From a headstone in Ireland

With deepest sympathy.

May God comfort you
and grant you peace
in this difficult time.

Our family grieves
the loss in yours, and
we send our love.

Though words cannot
express the thoughts
the heart would like
to say, still, may you
know that others care
and sympathize today.

**May you find
the strength to
face tomorrow
in the love
that surrounds
you today.**

*I want to comfort you and don't know where to begin …
but if I could take away the pain, I would.*

May the beautiful memories that fill your heart help to bring you comfort.

In this time of sadness, our thoughts are with you.

May you be comforted this day with the love of those around you.

May God's peace and strength shelter you in this time of sorrow.

Your loved one will always be as close as a memory, and the God of all comfort as close as a prayer.

Loss leaves us empty —but learn not to close your heart and mind in grief. Allow life to replenish you. When sorrow comes it seems impossible —but new joys wait to fill the void.

—Pam Brown

May you feel the healing touch of every thought and prayer that's sent with love and sympathy from friends who truly care.

It's hard to find the words that might bring comfort to you right now … we just hope you'll remember how much we care, and that our thoughts are with you.

Caring about your sorrow and remembering you in prayer.

May it be a comfort for you to know that your loss is shared by those who care about you very much.

May love, time and memories soften your sadness and bring you peace.

In time, your special memories will bring comfort to your soul and peace to your heart.

May you find comfort in friendship and strength in love.

May you find strength in the love that surrounds you.

May you find comfort in knowing our
thoughts and prayers are with you.

Our love goes out to you in this time of sadness.

May God's love heal your sorrow, and may his peace
replace your heartache with warm and loving memories.

May the promise of God's Word be your hope today,
your peace tomorrow and your comfort always.

*May God,
who calls dear
ones home ... enfold
you with his love
and send his comfort.*

With deepest
sympathy and
caring thoughts
as you honor a
treasured life.

Please count us among the many who are thinking of you today
with understanding and sympathy too deep for words to say.

In this difficult time may you find the kindness of friends to comfort you, compassion to warm and sustain you, and the unfailing peace of Jesus to bring peace to your heart.

Please count us among the many who are thinking of you today with understanding and sympathy too deep for words to say.

It's so hard to find the right words, but I hope you'll know somehow, my sympathy and very warmest thoughts are with you now.

With our sympathy ... a special life has passed from our sight, but never from our hearts.

May you find comfort in the sorrow that you bear, knowing there are many hearts that understand and care.

Today it's difficult to see beyond the sorrow … may your memories help comfort your tomorrows.

In all the world, there couldn't be a better friend than you.

No duty is more urgent than that of returning thanks.

—James Allen

Thank you for all the love and kindness that you share.

I'm grateful for what you've done for me!

Thank you for believing in me.

We can only be said to be alive in those moments when our hearts are conscious of our treasures

—Thornton Wilder

A kind heart is a fountain of gladness making everything in its vicinity freshen into smiles.

—Washington Irving

Love and kindness are never wasted. They always make a difference. They bless the one who receives them, and they bless you, the giver. —Barbara De Angelis

Thank You

Thank you from the bottom of my heart.

Gratitude: cause of happiness or joy.

I always appreciate your wisdom and honesty. Thanks for being such a great friend.

A little Consideration, a little Thought for Others, makes all the difference.

—Winnie the Pooh (A. A. Milne)

I can no other answer make, but thanks, and thanks.

—William Shakespeare

Thank you for the help, hope and kindness you have shared.

Your kindness was so appreciated.

You've touched my heart.

What a nice thing to do! Thank you so much!

You listen, you give me great advice, and you care. Thanks for being the best friend a girl could have.

Thank you for making me feel so welcome.

Gratitude is the fairest blossom that springs from the soul.

To thoughtful you from grateful me … thank you.

Two simple words that come with so much gratitude … thank you.

The smallest act of kindness is worth more than the grandest intention.

—Oscar Wilde

Not what we give,
But what we share;
For the gift
without the giver
Is bare.

—James Russell Lowell

What can I say?
You made
my day.

Thank You

Your loving, kind heart makes this world a better place.

The only people with whom you should try to get even are those who have helped you.

—John E. Southard

Wishing you a day as warm as your heart.

It's nice to be important, but it's more important to be nice.

I would thank you from the bottom of my heart, but for you my heart has no bottom.

Just sending you some "warm fuzzies."

I can't spell success without U.

Thank you for your thoughtfulness and kindness.

Kindness is the language which the deaf can hear, and the blind can see.

—Mark Twain

Hospitality and you go together. Thank you.

You are always so kind.

Thank you for all the things you do for me.

When I count my blessings I count you twice!

Thankful am I for your goodness to me.

Often in the quiet of the day, my thoughts are of the many kindnesses you have shown me.

You make my world a beautiful place to live and grow.

You have touched so many hearts.

The things you do are sweeter than apple pie. Thank you so much!

Thank You

Thank you for caring.

Appreciation: a just valuation or estimate of merit,
worth, weight, etc.; recognition of excellence.

Your kindness is such a blessing.

How thoughtful! Thanks so much!

Your thoughtfulness warms my heart.

Blessings brighten when we count them.

How beautiful
a day can be
when kindness
touches it!
—George Elliston

It's just like you to be so nice!

The hardest arithmetic to master is that which enables us to count our blessings. —Eric Hoffer

With joyful thanks for your kindness.

How far that little candle throws his beams!
So shines a good deed in a weary world.

—William Shakespeare

Something that has always puzzled me all my life is why, when I am in special need of help, the good deed is usually done by somebody on whom I have no claim.

—William Feather

I'm so thankful for our friendship, which blooms brighter every day.

Thank you for the wonderful encouragement and caring you share every day.

One can pay back the loan of gold, but one dies forever in debt to those who are kind.

—Malayan proverb

Thank you for being my sunshine every day.

You're so thoughtful ...
thank you so much.

Gratitude is the memory of the heart.

—Jean Baptiste Massieu

YOUR QUOTES

_____

_____

_____

_____

_____

_____

_____

_____

_____

_____

_____

_____

_____

_____

PROJECT CREDITS AND SOURCE LIST

A special thank you goes to Adrienne Kennedy from My Sentiments Exactly! for providing us with the cards featured on our chapter intro pages. Below is a list of products used to create each of these projects.

Birthdays, pg. 6
Sources: Printed paper and die cuts from Tinkering Ink; rub-on transfers from MSE!; rhinestone stickers from Heidi Swapp.

Children, pg. 18
Sources: Printed papers from Crate Paper Inc.; stamps from MSE!; flower from Making Memories; ribbon from Creative Impressions.

Christmas, pg. 26
Sources: Printed papers and rub-on transfers from Tinkering Ink; stamps from MSE!; rhinestone stickers from Heidi Swapp; ribbons from May Arts and Creative Impressions.

Encouragement, pg. 38
Sources: Printed papers from Tinkering Ink; rub-on transfers from MSE!; flower from Heidi Swapp; ribbon from May Arts.

Family, pg. 52
Sources: Printed papers from Tinkering Ink; stamps from MSE!; chipboard paisley shape from Fancy Pants Designs; glitter pen from Sakura of America; brads from Creative Impressions.

Friendship, pg. 58
Sources: Printed papers from Tinkering Ink; stamps from MSE!; flower from Prima Marketing Inc.; metal-edge tag and rhinestone brad from Making Memories; ribbons from May Arts.

Gardens, pg. 72
Sources: Printed papers and rub-on transfers from Tinkering Ink; stamps from MSE!; mini brads from Creative Impressions; ribbon from American Crafts Inc.

Get Well, pg. 78
Sources: Printed papers from Crate Paper Inc.; stamps from MSE!; flowers and big brad from Bazzill Basics Paper Inc.; ribbon from Creative Impressions.

Holidays, pg. 84
Sources: Printed papers from A2Z Essentials; rub-on transfers from MSE! and Tinkering Ink; acrylic oval tag from Tinkering Ink; stamps from MSE!; flower button from Autumn Leaves; rhinestone brad from Making Memories; ribbon from Creative Impressions.

Humorous, pg. 98
Sources: Printed papers from Tinkering Ink; stamp from MSE!; clear button from Making Memories; ribbon from May Arts.

Love, pg. 104
Sources: Printed papers from Crate Paper Inc.; rub-on transfers from MSE!; rhinestone paisley from me & my BIG ideas; glitter button from Autumn Leaves; flowers from Prima Marketing Inc. and Making Memories; mini tag from K&Company.

Miscellaneous, pg. 114
Sources: Printed papers from Tinkering Ink; stamps from MSE!; mini safety pin and metal tag from Creative Impressions; epoxy stickers from Cloud 9 Design; grommet from Making Memories; ribbon from May Arts.

Occasions, pg. 122
Sources: Printed papers from Tinkering Ink; rub-on transfers from MSE!; rhinestone sticker from Heidi Swapp; brads from Creative Impressions.

Parenting, pg. 132
Sources: Printed papers from Tinkering Ink; rub-on transfers from MSE!; loop eyelet from Karen Foster Design; ribbon buckle from Making Memories; charm from AMM; ribbon from Creative Impressions.

Religious, pg. 144
Sources: Printed papers from Tinkering Ink; stamps from MSE!; chipboard tag from BasicGrey; flowers from Prima Marketing Inc.; jewels from Heidi Swapp; eyelet snaps from Making Memories; ribbon from Creative Impressions.

Seasons, pg. 150
Sources: Printed papers from Fancy Pants Designs; stamps from MSE!; glitter brads from K&Company; frame from BasicGrey; flower from Prima Marketing Inc.; ribbon from May Arts.

Sympathy, pg. 156
Sources: Printed papers from Crate Paper Inc.; stamp from MSE!; pearl brads from K&Company.

Thank You, pg. 166
Sources: Printed papers and rub-on transfers from Tinkering Ink; stamps from MSE!; big brad from Bazzill Basics Paper Inc.; jewels from Heidi Swapp and Doodlebug Design Inc.

BUYER'S GUIDE

A2Z Essentials
(419) 663-2869
www.geta2z.com

American Crafts Inc.
(801) 226-0747
www.americancrafts.com

AMM/Advantus Corp.
(904) 482-0092
www.allmymemories.com

Autumn Leaves
(800) 588-6707
www.autumnleaves.com

BasicGrey
(801) 544-1116
www.basicgrey.com

Bazzill Basics Paper Inc.
(480) 558-8557
www.bazzillbasics.com

Cloud 9 Design
(866) 348-5661
www.cloud9design.biz

Crate Paper Inc.
(801) 798-8996
www.cratepaper.com

Creative Impressions
www.creativeimpressions.com

Doodlebug Design Inc.
www.doodlebug.ws

Fancy Pants Designs
(801) 779-3212
www.fancypantsdesigns.com

Heidi Swapp/Advantus Corp.
(904) 482-0092
www.heidiswapp.com

K&Company
(888) 244-2083
www.kandcompany.com

Karen Foster Design
(801) 326-1373
www.scrapbookpaper.com

Making Memories
(801) 294-0430
www.makingmemories.com

May Arts
www.mayarts.com

me & my BIG ideas
(949) 583-2065
www.meandmybigideas.com

MSE!
(719) 260-6001
www.sentiments.com

Prima Marketing Inc.
(909) 627-5532
www.primamarketinginc.com

Sakura of America
www.sakuraofamerica.com

Tinkering Ink
(877) scrap-ti (727-2784)
www.tinkeringink.com

The Buyer's Guide listings are provided as a service to our readers and should not be considered an endorsement from this publication.